The nature of the kingdom, or church, of Christ. A sermon preach'd before the King, at the Royal Chapel at St. James's, on Sunday March 31, 1717. By ... Benjamin Lord Bishop of Bangor. ... The fifth edition.

Benjamin Hoadly

Eighteenth Century
Collections Online
Print Editions

Gale ECCO Print Editions

Relive history with *Eighteenth Century Collections Online*, now available in print for the independent historian and collector. This series includes the most significant English-language and foreign-language works printed in Great Britain during the eighteenth century, and is organized in seven different subject areas including literature and language; medicine, science, and technology; and religion and philosophy. The collection also includes thousands of important works from the Americas.

The eighteenth century has been called "The Age of Enlightenment." It was a period of rapid advance in print culture and publishing, in world exploration, and in the rapid growth of science and technology – all of which had a profound impact on the political and cultural landscape. At the end of the century the American Revolution, French Revolution and Industrial Revolution, perhaps three of the most significant events in modern history, set in motion developments that eventually dominated world political, economic, and social life.

In a groundbreaking effort, Gale initiated a revolution of its own: digitization of epic proportions to preserve these invaluable works in the largest online archive of its kind. Contributions from major world libraries constitute over 175,000 original printed works. Scanned images of the actual pages, rather than transcriptions, recreate the works *as they first appeared.*

Now for the first time, these high-quality digital scans of original works are available via print-on-demand, making them readily accessible to libraries, students, independent scholars, and readers of all ages.

For our initial release we have created seven robust collections to form one the world's most comprehensive catalogs of 18th century works.

Initial Gale ECCO Print Editions collections include:

History and Geography
Rich in titles on English life and social history, this collection spans the world as it was known to eighteenth-century historians and explorers. Titles include a wealth of travel accounts and diaries, histories of nations from throughout the world, and maps and charts of a world that was still being discovered. Students of the War of American Independence will find fascinating accounts from the British side of conflict.

Social Science
Delve into what it was like to live during the eighteenth century by reading the first-hand accounts of everyday people, including city dwellers and farmers, businessmen and bankers, artisans and merchants, artists and their patrons, politicians and their constituents. Original texts make the American, French, and Industrial revolutions vividly contemporary.

Medicine, Science and Technology
Medical theory and practice of the 1700s developed rapidly, as is evidenced by the extensive collection, which includes descriptions of diseases, their conditions, and treatments. Books on science and technology, agriculture, military technology, natural philosophy, even cookbooks, are all contained here.

Literature and Language
Western literary study flows out of eighteenth-century works by Alexander Pope, Daniel Defoe, Henry Fielding, Frances Burney, Denis Diderot, Johann Gottfried Herder, Johann Wolfgang von Goethe, and others. Experience the birth of the modern novel, or compare the development of language using dictionaries and grammar discourses.

Religion and Philosophy
The Age of Enlightenment profoundly enriched religious and philosophical understanding and continues to influence present-day thinking. Works collected here include masterpieces by David Hume, Immanuel Kant, and Jean-Jacques Rousseau, as well as religious sermons and moral debates on the issues of the day, such as the slave trade. The Age of Reason saw conflict between Protestantism and Catholicism transformed into one between faith and logic -- a debate that continues in the twenty-first century.

Law and Reference
This collection reveals the history of English common law and Empire law in a vastly changing world of British expansion. Dominating the legal field is the *Commentaries of the Law of England* by Sir William Blackstone, which first appeared in 1765. Reference works such as almanacs and catalogues continue to educate us by revealing the day-to-day workings of society.

Fine Arts
The eighteenth-century fascination with Greek and Roman antiquity followed the systematic excavation of the ruins at Pompeii and Herculaneum in southern Italy; and after 1750 a neoclassical style dominated all artistic fields. The titles here trace developments in mostly English-language works on painting, sculpture, architecture, music, theater, and other disciplines. Instructional works on musical instruments, catalogs of art objects, comic operas, and more are also included.

The BiblioLife Network

This project was made possible in part by the BiblioLife Network (BLN), a project aimed at addressing some of the huge challenges facing book preservationists around the world. The BLN includes libraries, library networks, archives, subject matter experts, online communities and library service providers. We believe every book ever published should be available as a high-quality print reproduction; printed on-demand anywhere in the world. This insures the ongoing accessibility of the content and helps generate sustainable revenue for the libraries and organizations that work to preserve these important materials.

The following book is in the "public domain" and represents an authentic reproduction of the text as printed by the original publisher. While we have attempted to accurately maintain the integrity of the original work, there are sometimes problems with the original work or the micro-film from which the books were digitized. This can result in minor errors in reproduction. Possible imperfections include missing and blurred pages, poor pictures, markings and other reproduction issues beyond our control. Because this work is culturally important, we have made it available as part of our commitment to protecting, preserving, and promoting the world's literature.

GUIDE TO FOLD-OUTS MAPS and OVERSIZED IMAGES

The book you are reading was digitized from microfilm captured over the past thirty to forty years. Years after the creation of the original microfilm, the book was converted to digital files and made available in an online database.

In an online database, page images do not need to conform to the size restrictions found in a printed book. When converting these images back into a printed bound book, the page sizes are standardized in ways that maintain the detail of the original. For large images, such as fold-out maps, the original page image is split into two or more pages

Guidelines used to determine how to split the page image follows:

• Some images are split vertically; large images require vertical and horizontal splits.
• For horizontal splits, the content is split left to right.
• For vertical splits, the content is split from top to bottom.
• For both vertical and horizontal splits, the image is processed from top left to bottom right.

The NATURE of the KINGDOM, or CHURCH, of CHRIST.

A

SERMON

Preach'd before the

KING,

AT THE

Royal Chapel at St. *James's*,
On SUNDAY *March* 31, 1717.

By the Right Reverend FATHER in GOD
BENJAMIN Lord Bishop of BANGOR.

Publish'd by His Majesty's Special Command.

The Fourth EDITION.

LONDON,
Printed for JAMES KNAPTON, at the *Crown*,
and TIMOTHY CHILDE, at the *White Hart*
in St. Paul's Church-yard. MDCCXVII.

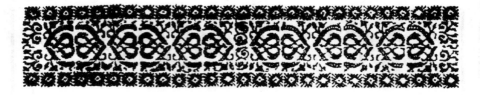

St. JOHN, xviii. 36.

Jesus answered, My Kingdom is not of this World.

ONE of those great Effects, which length of Time is seen to bring along with it, is the Alteration of the Meaning annexed to certain Sounds. The Signification of a Word, well known and understood by Those who first made use of it, is very insensibly varied, by passing thrô many Mouths, and by being taken and given by Multitudes, in common Discourse; till it often comes to stand for a Complication of Notions, as distant from the original Intention of it, nay, as contradictory to it, as Darkness is to Light. The Ignorance and Weakness of Some, and

A 2   the

the Paffions and Bad Defigns of Others, are the great Inftruments of this Evil: which, even when it feems to affect only indifferent Matters, ought in reafon to be oppofed, as it tends in it's nature to confound Men's Notions in weightier Points; but, when it hath once invaded the moft Sacred and Important Subjects, ought, in Duty, to be refifted with a more open and undifguifed Zeal, as what toucheth the very Vitals of all that is good, and is juft going to take from Men's Eyes the Boundaries of Right and Wrong.

The only Cure for this *Evil*, in Cafes of fo great Concern, is to have recourfe to the Originals of Things: to the Law of Reafon, in thofe Points which can be traced back thither; and to the Declarations of *Jefus Chrift*, and his immediate Followers, in fuch Matters, as took their Rife folely from thofe Declarations. For the Cafe is plainly this, that Words and Sounds have had fuch an Effect, (not upon the Nature of Things, which is unmoveable, but) upon the Minds of Men in

thinking

thinking of them; that the very same Word remaining, (which at firſt truly repreſented One certain Thing,) by having Multitudes of new inconſiſtent Ideas, in every Age, and every Year, added to it, becomes it ſelf the greateſt Hindrance to the true underſtanding of the Nature of the Thing firſt intended by it.

For Inſtance, *Religion*, in St. *James's* Days, was Virtue and Integrity, as to our ſelves, and Charity and Beneficence to others; before *God*, even the *Father*. *Ja.* i. 27. By Degrees, it is come to ſigniﬁy, in moſt of the Countries throughout the whole World, the Performance of every thing almoſt, except Virtue and Charity; and particularly, a punctual Exactneſs in a Regard to particular *Times, Places, Forms,* and *Modes*, diverſiﬁed according to the various Humours of Men; recommended and practiſed under the avowed Name of *External Religion: Two Words*, which, in the Senſe fix'd upon them by many Chriſtians, *God hath put aſunder*; and which therefore, *no Man ſhould join together.*

gether. And accordingly, the Notion of a *Religious Man* differs in every Country, just as much as *Times, Places, Ceremonies, Imaginary Austerities,* and all other *Outward Circumstances,* are different and various: Whereas in truth, thô a Man, truly *Religious* in other Respects, may make use of such Things; yet, they cannot be the least part of his *Religion,* properly so call'd, any more than his Food, or his Raiment, or any other Circumstance of his Life.

Thus likewise, the *Worship* of *God,* to be paid by Christians, was, in *our Saviour's* time, and in his own plain Words, the Worship of the Father *in Spirit and Truth;* and this declared to be one great End proposed in the *Christian Dispensation: The Hour cometh, and now is, when the true Worshippers shall Worship the Father in Spirit and in Truth: for the Father seeketh such to worship him.* John iv. 23. But the *Notion* of it is become quite another thing: and in many *Christian Countries,* that which still retains the Name of the *Worship* of *God,* is indeed the Neglect,

lect, and the Diminution of the Father; and the Worship of other Beings besides, and more than, the *Father*. And this, performed in such a manner, as that any *indifferent Spectator* would conclude, that neither the Consciences nor Understandings of Men, neither *Spirit* nor *Truth*, were at all concerned in the Matter; or rather, that they had been banish'd from it by an express Command. In the mean time, the *Word*, or *Sound*, still remains the same in Discourse. The whole Lump of indigested, and inconsistent Notions and Practices; Every thing that is solemnly said, or done, when the *Worship* of *God* is profess'd, is equally cover'd under that *general Name*; and, by the help of using the same *Original Word*, passeth easily for the *Thing* it self. Again,

Prayer, in all our *Lord's* Directions about it, and particularly in that *Form*, which He himself taught his Followers, was a calm, undisturbed, *Address* to *God*, under the Notion of a *Father*, expressing those Sentiments and Wishes before

before Him, which every sincere Mind
ought to have.   But the same *Word*, by
the help of Men, and voluminous Rules
of Art, is come to signify *Heat* and
Flame, in such a manner, and to such
a degree, that, a Man may be in the
best Disposition in the World, and yet
not be *devout* enough to *Pray:* and
many an honest Person hath been per-
plex'd, by this Means, with Doubts
and Fears of being uncapable of *Pray-
ing*, for want of an *intenseness* of *Heat*,
which hath no more relation to the
Duty, than a Man's being in a *Fever*
hath, to the Sincerity of his Professions,
or Addresses to any *Earthly Prince.*

Once more, the *Love of God*, and
of *our Saviour*, was at first, in his own
Words, and those of St. *John*, many
times repeated, the *keeping his Com-
mandments, or doing his Will.*   Joh. 14.
15, 21, 23. *ch.* 15. 10. I Joh. 2. 5. *ch.* 5.
3. II *Joh.* 6. But the *Notion* of it was, it
seems, left very jejune; and so hath
been improved by his *later Followers*, till
the same *Name*, still kept up in the Language of *Christians*, is far removed from
the

he *Thing* principally and first intend-
·d ; and is come by degrees to signify
a violent *Paßion, Commotion,* and *Ecsta-*
,y, venting it self in such sort of Expre-
·fions and Diforders, as other *Paßions*
do: and this regulated and defined, by
fuch a Variety of Imaginations, that
an ordinary *Chriftian,* with the utmoft
Sincerity in his Heart, is filled with nothing but eternal Sufpicions, Doubts,
and Perplexities, whether he hath any
thing of the true *Love* of *God,* or not.

I have mentioned thefe *Particulars,*
not only to fhew the Evil it felf; and
to how great a Degree the *Nature* of
Things hath fuffered in the Opinions of
Men, by the Alteration of the Senfe of
the fame *Words* and *Sounds:* but to give
you Occafion to obferve, that there can
be no Cure for it, in *Chriftians,* but to
go back to the *New Teftament* it felf; becaufe *there* alone we fhall find the Original Intention of fuch Words ; or the
Nature of the Things defign'd to be fig-
nified by them, declared and fixed by
our *Lord,* or his *Apoftles* from him, by

B   fome

fome fuch Marks, as may, if we will attend to them, guide and guard us in our Notions of thofe Matters, in which we are moft of all concern'd.

It is with this View, that I have cho-fen thofe *Words*, in which our *Lord* himfelf declared the Nature of *his own Kingdom.* This *Kingdom* of *Chrift*, is the fame with the *Church* of *Chrift.*   And the *Notion* of the *Church* of *Chrift*, which, at firft, was only the Number, fmall or great, of Thofe who believed *Him* to be the *Meffiah*; or of Thofe who fub-jected themfelves to *Him*, as their *King*, in the Affair of *Religion*; having fince that Time been fo diverfified by the va-rious *Alterations* it hath undergone, that it is almoft impoffible fo much as to number up the many *inconfiftent Images* that have come, by daily Additions, to be united together in it : nothing, I think, can be more ufeful, than to con-fider the fame thing, under fome other *Image*, which hath not been fo much u-fed; nor confequently fo much defaced. And fince the *Image* of *His Kingdom*, is

That

That, under which our Lord himſelf choſe to repreſent it: We may be ſure that, if we ſincerely examine our Notion of his *Church*, by what He ſaith of his *Kingdom*, that *it is not of this World*, we ſhall exclude out of it, every thing that he would have excluded; and then, what remains will be true, pure, and uncorrupted. And what I have to ſay, in order to this, will be comprehended under Two *General Heads.*

I. As the *Church* of *Chriſt* is the *Kingdom of Chriſt*, *He* himſelf is *King*: and in this it is implied, that *He* is himſelf the ſole *Law-giver* to his *Subjects*, and himſelf the ſole *Judge* of their *Behaviour*, in the Affairs of *Conſcience* and *Eternal Salvation.* And in this Senſe therefore, *His Kingdom is not of this World*; that He hath, in thoſe Points, left behind Him, no viſible, humane *Authority*; no *Vicegerents*, who can be ſaid properly to ſupply his Place; no *Interpreters*, upon whom his Subjects are abſolutely to depend; no *Judges* over the Conſciences or Religion of his Peo-

B 2 ple.

ple.   For if this were so, that any such absolute *Vicegerent Authority*, either for the making *new Laws*, or interpreting *Old* Ones, or *judging* his *Subjects*, in *Religious* Matters, were lodged in any Men upon Earth, the Consequence would be, that what still retains the Name of the *Church* of *Christ*, would not be the *Kingdom of Christ*, but the *Kingdom* of those Men, vested with such *Authority*. For, whoever hath such an *Authority* of making Laws, is so far a *King*: and whoever can add new Laws to those of *Christ*, equally obligatory, is as truly a *King*, as *Christ* himself is: Nay, whoever hath an *absolute Authority* to *interpret* any written, or spoken Laws; it is *He*, who is truly the *Law-giver*, to all Intents and Purposes; and not the Person who first wrote, or spoke them.

In humane Society, the *Interpretation* of *Laws* may, of necessity, be lodged, in some Cases, in the Hands of Those who were not originally the *Legislators*. But this is not *absolute*; nor of bad

Consequence

Confequence to *Society:* becaufe the *Legiflators* can refume the *Interpretation* into their own Hands, as they are Witneffes to what paffes in the World ; and as They can, and will, fenfibly interpofe in all thofe Cafes, in which their Interpofition becomes neceffary. And therefore, They are ftill properly the *Legiflators.* But it is otherwife in *Religion,* or the *Kingdom* of *Chrift.* He himfelf never interpofeth, fince his firft Promulgation of his *Law*, either to convey *Infallibility* to Such as pretend to handle it over again; or to affert the true *Interpretation* of it, amidft the various and contradictory Opinions of Men about it. If *He* did certainly thus interpofe, He himfelf would ftill be the *Legiflator.* But, as *He* doth not; if fuch an abfolute *Authority* be once lodged with Men, under the Notion of *Interpreters,* They then become the *Legiflators,* and not *Chrift*; and *They* rule in their own *Kingdom,* and not in *His.*

It is the fame thing, as to Rewards and Punifhments, to carry forward the great

great End of his *Kingdom*. If any Men
upon Earth have a *Right* to add to the
Sanctions of his *Laws*; that is, to in-
creafe the Number, or alter the Nature,
of the *Rewards* and *Punifhments* of his
Subjects, in Matters of Confcience, or
Salvation : They are fo far *Kings* in his
ftead; and Reign in *their own* Kingdom,   and not in *His*.   So it is, whenever They erect *Tribunals*, and exercife
a *Judgment* over the Confciences of
Men ; and affume to Themfelves the
Determination of fuch Points, as cannot be determined, but by *One* who
knows the Hearts; or, when They
make any of their own Declarations,
or Decifions, to concern and affect the
State of Chrift's Subjects, with regard
to the Favour of God: this is fo far,
the taking *Chrift's Kingdom* out of *His*
Hands, and placing it in their own.

Nor is this matter at all made better
by their declaring Themfelves to be *Vicegerents*, or *Law makers*, or *Judges*, under
Chrift, in order to carry on the Ends of
his Kingdom. For it comes to this at laft,
                                        fince

since it doth not seem fit to Christ himself to interpose so as to prevent or reme-
dy all their mistakes and contradictions,
that, if They have this power of interpreting, or adding, Laws, and judging
Men, in such a sense, that *Christians*
shall be indispensably and absolutely o-
bliged to obey those *Laws*, and to submit to those *Decisions*; I say, if They
have this power lodged with them, then
the *Kingdom*, in which they rule, is not
the Kingdom of *Christ*, but of *Themselves*; *He* doth not rule in it, but *They*:
And, whether They happen to agree
with him, or to differ from Him, as
long as they are the *Law-givers*, and
Judges, without any Interposition from
Christ, either to guide or correct their
Decisions, *They* are *Kings* of this *Kingdom*, and not *Christ Jesus*.

If therefore, the *Church* of *Christ* be
the *Kingdom* of *Christ*; it is essential to
it, that *Christ* himself be the Sole *Law-
giver*, and Sole *Judge* of his Subjects, in
all points relating to the favour or dis-
pleasure

pleasure of *Almighty God*; and that All His *Subjects*, in what Station soever they may be, are equally *Subjects* to *Him*; and that No One of them, any more than Another, hath *Authority*, either to make *New Laws* for *Christ's* Subjects; or to impose a sense upon the *Old* Ones, which is the same thing; or to *Judge*, Censure, or Punish, the Servants of *Another Master*, in matters relating purely to *Conscience*, or *Salvation*. If any Person hath any other Notion, either thro' a long Use of Words with Inconsistent Meanings, or thro' a negligence of Thought; let him but ask himself, whether the *Church* of *Christ* be the Kingdom of *Christ*, or not: And, if it be, whether this Notion of it doth not absolutely exclude all other *Legislators* and *Judges*, in matters relating to Conscience, or the favour of God; or, whether it can be *His* Kingdom, if any Mortal Men have such a Power of *Legislation* and *Judgment* in it. This *Enquiry* will bring Us back to the first, which is the only True, Account of the *Church* of *Christ*, or
the

the *Kingdom* of *Christ*, in the mouth of a Christian: That it is the Number of Men, whether Small or Great, whether Dispersed or united, who truly and sincerely are Subjects to *Jesus Christ* alone, as their *Law-giver* and *Judge*, in matters relating to the Favour of God, and their *Eternal Salvation.*

II. The next principal point is, that, if the *Church* be the *Kingdom* of *Christ*; and this *Kingdom be not of this World*: this must appear from the Nature and End of the *Laws* of Christ; and of those Rewards and Punishments, which are the *Sanctions* of his *Laws*. Now his *Laws* are Declarations, relating to the Favour of God in another State after this. They are Declarations of those Conditions to be perform'd, in this World, on our part, without which God will not make us Happy in that to come. And they are almost All general Appeals to the *Will* of that God, to his *Nature*, known by the Common Reason of Mankind; and to the imitation of that *Nature*, which must be our *Perfection*. The *Keeping his Com-*

C *mandments*

mandments is declared the *Way* to Life; and the *doing his Will*, the Entrance into the *Kingdom of Heaven*. The being *Subjects* to *Christ*, is to this very End, that We may the better and more effectually perform the *Will* of *God*. The *Laws* of this *Kingdom*, therefore, as *Christ* left them, have nothing of *this* World in their view; no Tendency, either to the Exaltation of *Some*, in worldly pomp and dignity, or to their absolute Dominion over the Faith and Religious conduct of *Others* of his Subjects; or to the erecting of any sort of *Temporal Kingdom*, under the Covert and Name of a *Spiritual* one.

The *Sanctions* of *Christ's Law* are *Rewards* and *Punishments*. But of what sort? Not the Rewards of this World; not the Offices, or Glories, of this State; not the pains of *Prisons*, *Banishments*, *Fines*, or any lesser and more *Moderate Penalties*, nay, not the much lesser *Negative Discouragements* that belong to *Humane Society*. He was far from thinking that *These* could be the Instruments of such a *Perswasion*, as He thought acceptable to God. But, as the Great End of

his

his *Kingdom*, was to guide Men to Happiness, after the short Images of it were over here below; so, He took his *Motives* from that place, where His *Kingdom* first began, and where it was at last to end; from those *Rewards* and *Punishments* in a future State, which had no relation to this World: And, to shew that his *Kingdom was not of this World*, all the *Sanctions* which He thought fit to give to *His Laws*, were *not of this World* at all.

St. *Paul* understood this so well, that He gives an Account of His own Conduct, and that of Others in the same Station, in these words, *Knowing the terrors of the Lord, we perswade men*: whereas, in too many *Christian Countries*, since his days, if Some, who profess to succeed *Him*, were to give an Account of their own Conduct, it must be in a quite contrary strain; *Knowing the terrors of this World, and having them in our power, We do, not perswade men, but force their outward Profession against their inward Perswasion.*

Now, wherever *this* is practis'd, whe-

ther

ther in a great degree, or a small, in *that* place there is so far a Change, from a *Kingdom* which is *not of this world*, to a *Kingdom* which *is of this world*. As soon as ever you hear of any of the *Engines* of *this world*, whether of the greater, or the lesser sort, you must immediately think that then, and so far, the *Kingdom of this world* takes place. For, if the very Essence of God's worship be Spirit and Truth, If *Religion* be *Virtue* and *Charity*, under the *Belief* of a Supreme Governour and Judge; if True Real *Faith* cannot be the effect of *Force*; and, if there can be no *Reward* where there is no *Willing Choice*: then, in all, or any of these Cases, to apply Force or Flattery, Worldy pleasure or pain; is to act contrary to the Interests of True *Religion*, as it is plainly opposite to the Maxims upon which *Christ* founded his Kingdom; who chose the *Motives* which are *not of this world*, to support a *Kingdom* which *is not of this world*.   And indeed, it is too visible to be hid, that wherever the *Rewards* and *Punishments* are changed, from future to present, from the World to

come

come, to the World now in poffeffion; there, the *Kingdom* founded by our *Saviour* is, in the Nature of it, fo far changed, that it is become, in fuch a degree, what He profeffed, *His Kingdom was not:* that is, *of this world*; of the fame fort with other Common *Earthly* Kingdoms, in which the *Rewards* are, Worldly Honours, Pofts, Offices, Pomp, Attendance, Dominion; and the Punifhments are, Prifons, Fines, Banifhments, Gallies and Racks; or fomething Lefs, of the fame fort.

If *thefe* can be the true fupports of a *Kingdom* which is *not of this World*; then Sincerity, and Hypocrify; Religion, and No Religion; Force, and Perfwafion; A Willing Choice, and a Terrified Heart; are become the fame things: Truth and Falfhood ftand in need of the fame methods, to propagate and fupport them; and our *Saviour* himfelf was little acquainted with the *Right* way of increafing the Number of fuch *Subjects*, as He wifhed for. If He had but at firft enlighten'd the *Powers* of *this World*, as He did St. *Paul*; and employed the *Sword* which

which They bore, and the *Favours* They had in their hands, to bring *Subjects* into his *Kingdom*; this had been an Expeditious and an effectual way, according to the Conduct of some of his professed Followers, to have had a Glorious and Extensive *Kingdom*, or *Church*. But this was not his Design; unless it could be compassed in quite a different way.

And therefore, when You see *Our Lord*, in *his* methods, so far removed from Those of Many of his Disciples; when You read Nothing, in his Doctrine about his own *Kingdom*, of taking in the Concerns of this World, and mixing them with those of Eternity; no Commands that the Frowns and Discouragements of this present State should in any Case attend upon Conscience and Religion; No Rules against the Enquiry of All His Subjects into his *Original Message* from Heaven; no Orders for the kind and charitable force of *Penalties*, or *Capital Punishments*, to make Men think and chuse aright; no Calling upon the *secular Arm*, whenever the *Magistrate* should become *Christian*, to inforce his Doctrines, or

to

to back his *Spiritual Authority*; but, on the contrary, as plain a Declaration as a few Words can make, that *His Kingdom is not of this World:* I say, when You see this, from the whole Tenor of the *Gospel,* so vastly opposite to Many who take his Name into their Mouths, the Question with you ought to be, Whether He did not know the Nature of his own *Kingdom,* or *Church,* better than Any since his Time? whether you can suppose, *He* left any such matters to be decided against *Himself,* and his own Express professions, and, whether if an *Angel from Heaven* should give you any Account of his *Kingdom,* contrary to what He himself hath done, it can be of any Weight, or Authority, with Christians.

I have now made some such observations, drawn from the *Church* being the *Kingdom* of *Christ,* and not of any *Men* in that *Kingdom;* from the *Nature* of his *Laws,* and from those *Rewards* and *Punishments,* which are the Sanctions of those Laws; as lead us naturally into the true *Notion* of the *Church,* or *Kingdom,* of *Christ,*

Chrift, by excluding out of it every *thing* inconfiftent with *His* being *King*, *Law-giver* and *Judge*; as well as with the Nature of His *Laws*, and of His promifes and Threatnings. I will only make *Two* or *Three* Obfervations, grounded upon this: And fo conclude. And

1. From what hath been faid it is very plain, in general, that the Groffeft Miftakes in Judgment, about the Nature of *Chrift*'s *Kingdom*, or *Church*, have arifen from hence, that Men have argued from Other vifible *Societies*, and Other Vifible *Kingdoms of this World*, to what ought to be Vifible, and Senfible, in *His Kingdom*: Conftantly leaving out of their *Notion*, the moft Effential Part of it, that *Chrift* is *King* in his own *Kingdom*; forgetting this *King* himfelf, becaufe He is not now feen by mortal Eyes; and Subftituting *Others* in his Place, as *Law-givers* and *Judges*, in the fame Points, in which *He* muft either *Alone*, or not at all, be *Law-giver* and *Judge*; not contented with fuch a *Kingdom* as He eftablifhed, and defires to reign in; but ur-

ging

ging and contending, that *His Kingdom* muſt be like *Other Kingdoms*. Whereas He hath poſitively warn'd them againſt any ſuch Arguings, by aſſuring Them that this *Kingdom* is *His Kingdom*, and that it is *not of this World*; and therefore that No *one* of *His Subjects* is *Lawgiver* and *Judge* over *Others* of them, in matters relating to *Salvation*, but *He* alone; and that We muſt not Frame our Ideas from the *Kingdoms of this World*, of what ought to be, in a viſible and ſenſible manner, in *His Kingdom*.

2. From what hath been ſaid it appears that the *Kingdom* of *Chriſt*, which is the *Church* of *Chriſt*, is the *Number* of Perſons who are Sincerely, and Willingly, *Subjects* to *Him*, as *Law-giver* and *Judge*, in all matters truly relating to Conſcience, or Eternal Salvation. And the more cloſe and immediate this Regard to *Him* is, the more certainly and the more evidently true it is, that They are of his *Kingdom*. This may appear fully to their own Satisfaction, if They have recourſe to *Him* himſelf, in the *Goſpel*;

D *if*

if They think it a fufficient Authority
that He hath declared the *Conditions* of
their *Salvation*, and that No Man upon
Earth hath any Authority to declare any
other, or to add one tittle to them; if
They refolve to perform what They fee,
He laith a ftrefs upon; and if They truft
no mortal, with the abfolute direction
of their *Confciences*, the pardon of their
Sins, or the determining of their Intereft
in God's favour; but wait for their *Judge*,
who alone can bring to light *the hid-
den things of darknefs.*

If They feel themfelves difpofed and
refolved to receive the Words of *Eternal
Life* from *Himfelf*; to take their *Faith*
from what He himfelf *once delivered,*
who knew better than All the reft of the
World what He required of his own
Subjects ; to direct their *Worfhip* by his
Rule, and their whole practice by the
General Law which He laid down : If
They feel themfelves in this difpofiti-
on, They may be very certain that They
are truly his *Subjects*, and Members of
his *Kingdom.* Nor need They envy the
Happinefs of *Others*, who may think it

a

a much more evident Mark of their be-
longing to the *Kingdom* of *Christ*, that
They have *other* Law-givers, and Judges, in *Christ's Religion*, besides *Jesus
Christ*; that They have recourse not to
his own Words, but the Words of *Others*
who profess to interpret them; that They
are ready to Submit to this *Interpretation*,
let it be what it will; that They have
set up to Themselves the *Idol* of an un-
intelligible *Authority*, both in *Belief*, and
Worship, and *Practice*; in Words, *under*
Jesus Christ, but in deed and in truth
over Him; as it removes the minds of
his *Subjects* from *Himself*, to Weak, and
passionate Men; and as it claims the
same Rule and Power in *his Kingdom*,
which He himself *alone* can have. But,

3. This will be *Another observation*,
that it evidently destroys the *Rule* and
Authority of *Jesus Christ*, as *King*, to set
up any Other *Authority* in *His Kingdom*, to
which His Subjects are indispensably and
absolutely obliged to Submit their Consciences, or their Conduct, in what is
properly called Religion. There are *some*

D 2 Pro-

Profeffed Chriftians, who contend open-
ly for fuch an *Authority*, as indifpenfably
obliges All around Them to *Unity* of
Profeffion; that is, to Profefs even what
They do not, what They cannot, believe
to be true. This founds fo grofsly, that
Others, who think They act a glorious
part in oppofing fuch an Enormity, are
very willing, for their own fakes, to re-
tain fuch an *Authority* as fhall oblige
Men, whatever They themfelves think,
though not to profefs what They do not
believe, yet, to forbear the *profeffion* and
publication of what They do believe, let
them believe it of never fo great Im-
portance.

Both thefe *Pretenfions* are founded upon the miftaken *Notion* of the *Peace*, as
well as *Authority*, of the *Kingdom*, that
is the *Church*, of *Chrift*. Which of them
is the moft infupportable to an honeft
and a Chriftian mind, I am not able to
fay: becaufe They both equally found
the *Authority* of the *Church* of *Chrift*, upon the ruines of Sincerity and Common
Honefty; and miftake *Stupidity* and *Sleep*,
for *Peace*; becaufe They would both
equally

equally have prevented *All Reformation* where it hath been, and will for ever prevent it where it is not already; and, in a word, becaufe both equally deveft *Jefus Chrift* of his *Empire* in *his own* Kingdom; fet the obedience of his *Subjects* loofe from *Himfelf*; and teach them to proftitute their *Confciences* at the feet of *Others*, who have no right in fuch a manner to trample upon them.

The *Peace* of *Chrift's Kingdom* is a manly and Reafonable *Peace*; built upon Charity, and Love, and mutual forbearance, and receiving one another, as God receives us. As for any other *Peace*; founded upon a Submiffion of our *Honefty*, as well as our *Underftandings*; it is falfely fo called. It is not the *Peace* of the *Kingdom* of *Chrift*; but the *Lethargy* of it : and a *Sleep unto Death*, when his *Subjects* fhall throw off their relation to *Him*; fix their fubjection to *Others*; and even in Cafes, where They have a right to fee, and where They think They fee, his Will otherwife, fhall fhut their Eyes and go blindfold at the Command of *Others*; becaufe thofe *Others*

are

are not pleas'd with their Enquiries into the Will of their great Lord and Judge.

To conclude, The *Church of Christ* is the *Kingdom of Christ*. He is *King* in his own Kingdom. He is Sole *Law-giver* to his Subjects, and Sole *Judge*, in matters relating to Salvation. His *Laws* and *Sanctions* are plainly fixed: and relate to the Favour of God; and not at all to the Rewards, or Penalties, of *this World*. All his Subjects are *equally* his Subjects; and, as such, *equally* without Authority to alter, to add to, or to *interpret*, his *Laws* so, as to claim the absolute Submission of *Others* to such *Interpretation*. And All are *His Subjects*, and in his Kingdom, who are ruled and governed by *Him*. Their *Faith* was *once* delivered by *Him*. The Conditions of their Happiness were *once* laid down by *Him*. The Nature of *God's Worship* was *once* peclared by *Him*. And it is easy to judge, whether of the Two is most becoming a *Subject* of the *Kingdom of Christ*, that is, a *Member* of his *Church*; to seek all these particulars in those plain and
                                        short

short Declarations of their *King* and *Law-giver* himself: or to hunt after Them thro' the infinite contradictions, the numberless perplexities, the endless disputes, of *Weak Men*, in several Ages, till the Enquirer himself is lost in the Labyrinth, and perhaps sits down in Despair, or Infidelity. If *Christ* be our *King*; let us shew our selves *Subjects* to *Him* alone, in the great affair of Conscience and Eternal Salvation : and, without fear of Man's judgment, live and act as becomes Those who wait for the appearance of an All-knowing and Impartial Judge; even *that King*, whose *Kingdom is not of this World.*

FINIS.

115

CPSIA information can be obtained
at www.ICGtesting.com
Printed in the USA
LVHW050849211122
733688LV00005B/146